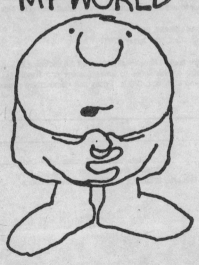

More Humor by Tom Wilson From SIGNET

A SIGNET BOOK

NEW AMERICAN LIBRARY

TIMES MIRROR

SIGNET TRADEMARK REG. U.S. PAT. OFF. AND FOREIGN COUNTRIES
REGISTERED TRADEMARK—MARCA REGISTRADA
HECHO EN CHICAGO, U.S.A.

SIGNET, SIGNET CLASSICS, MENTOR, PLUME, MERIDIAN AND NAL
BOOKS are published by The New American Library, Inc.,
1633 Broadway, New York, New York 10019

FIRST SIGNET PRINTING, SEPTEMBER, 1975

13   14

PRINTED IN THE UNITED STATES OF AMERICA

dedicated to YOU

...and all the other
ZIGGYS in the world...

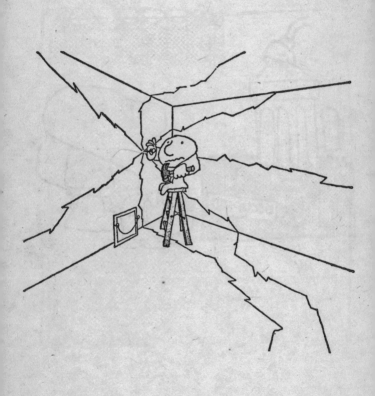

EVERY ZIGGY NEEDS A FRIEND

ZiGGY FaCeS LiFe

...IT ALWAYS GIVES ME KIND OF A SECURE FEELING TO FIND MY NAME IN THE TELEPHONE BOOK

YOU REALLY KNOW YOUR
LIFE IS MISSING SOMETHING
WHEN YOU FIND YOURSELF
WATCHING YOUR CLOTHES
DRYER ON SPIN CYCLE FOR
EXCITEMENT.....•••••

..i COULD DO MORE WITH MY LIFE... MAYBE EVEN BECOME AN ADVENTURER... ..SAILING OFF INTO UNCHARTED SEAS WITH THE SALT SPRAY IN MY FACE AND THE WIND AT MY BACK... DISCOVERING NEW WORLDS...
...IF I COULD ONLY GET OUT OF THIS CHAIR!!
TomWilson

AFTER YOU'RE ALL
GROWN UP... iT'S REALLY
DepReSSiNG WHEN YOU
REALiZe THAT YOU'RE NOT
ANY OF THE THINGS YOU
WANTeD TO Be WHEN YOU
GReW UP !!!

SOLITUDE IS A PEACE OF MIND
THAT COMES FROM WITHIN

..IT'S A QUIET SECLUSION
THAT CALMS THE SOUL

..IT'S A TIME OF SILENCE
AND CONTEMPLATION

..IT'S A
BIG DRAG !!

HURRY, HURRY, HURRY!
BUY THESE BOOKS!

6

Only 12,256,677 copies of these treasured classics left in stock.

☐ Al Jaffee Gags   (095464—$1.75)

☐ AL Jaffee Gags Again   (095839—$1.75)

☐ Al Jaffee Blows His Mind   (111907—$2.25)

☐ More Mad's Snappy Answers to Stupid Questions by Al Jaffee.   (067401—$1.25)

☐ Al Jaffee's Next Book   (113772—$1.50)

☐ Rotten Rhymes and Other Crimes by Nick Meglin. Illustrated by Al Jaffee.   (078918—$1.25)

☐ Al Jaffee Bombs Again   (116062—$1.50)

☐ Al Jaffee Draws A Crowd   (092759—$1.50)

☐ Al Jaffee Sinks to A New Low   (097572—$1.75)

☐ Al Jaffee Meets His End   (113179—$1.50)*

☐ Al Jaffee Goes Bananas   (112857—$1.95)

☐ Al Jaffee Meets Willie Weirdie   (110889—$1.95)*

☐ Al Jaffee Blows A Fuse   (095499—$1.75)

☐ Al Jaffee Gets His Just Desserts   (098382—$1.50)

☐ Al Jaffee Hogs the Show   (099087—$1.95)*

☐ Al Jaffee: Dead or Alive   (094948—$1.75)*

☐ Al Jaffee Fowls His Nest   (097416—$1.95)*

☐ The Ghoulish Book of Weird Records by Al Jaffee.   (112342—$1.50)*

*Price slightly higher in Canada

Buy them at your local

bookstore or use coupon

on next page for ordering.

More Hilarious Humor from SIGNET